Color By Number Adult Coloring Book of Spring Birds

This Spring Birds Coloring Book belongs to:

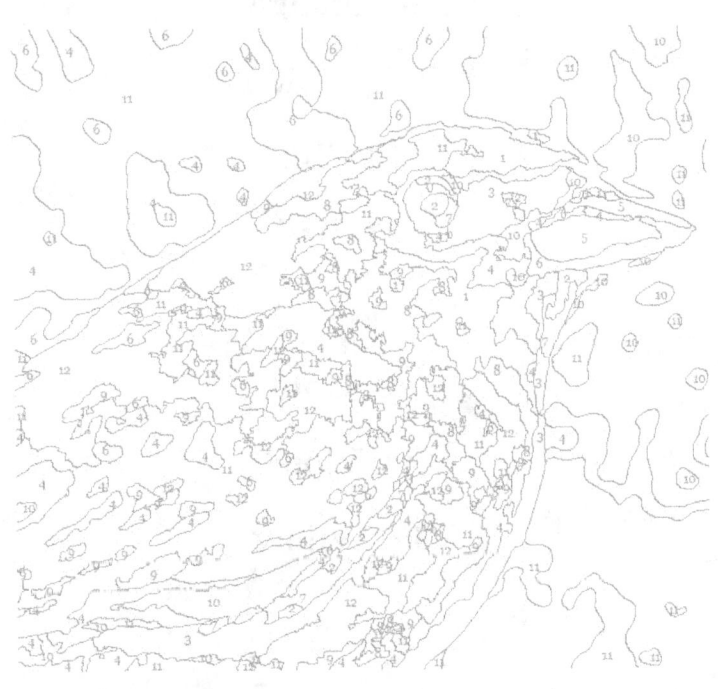

Copyright © 2019 Spring Birds Coloring Books

1. Black
2. Green
3. Blue
4. Brown
5. Purple
6. Light Blue
7. Light Green
8. Orange
9. Dark Red
10. Pink
11. Red
12. Dark Green
13. Gold
14. Violet
15. Yellow

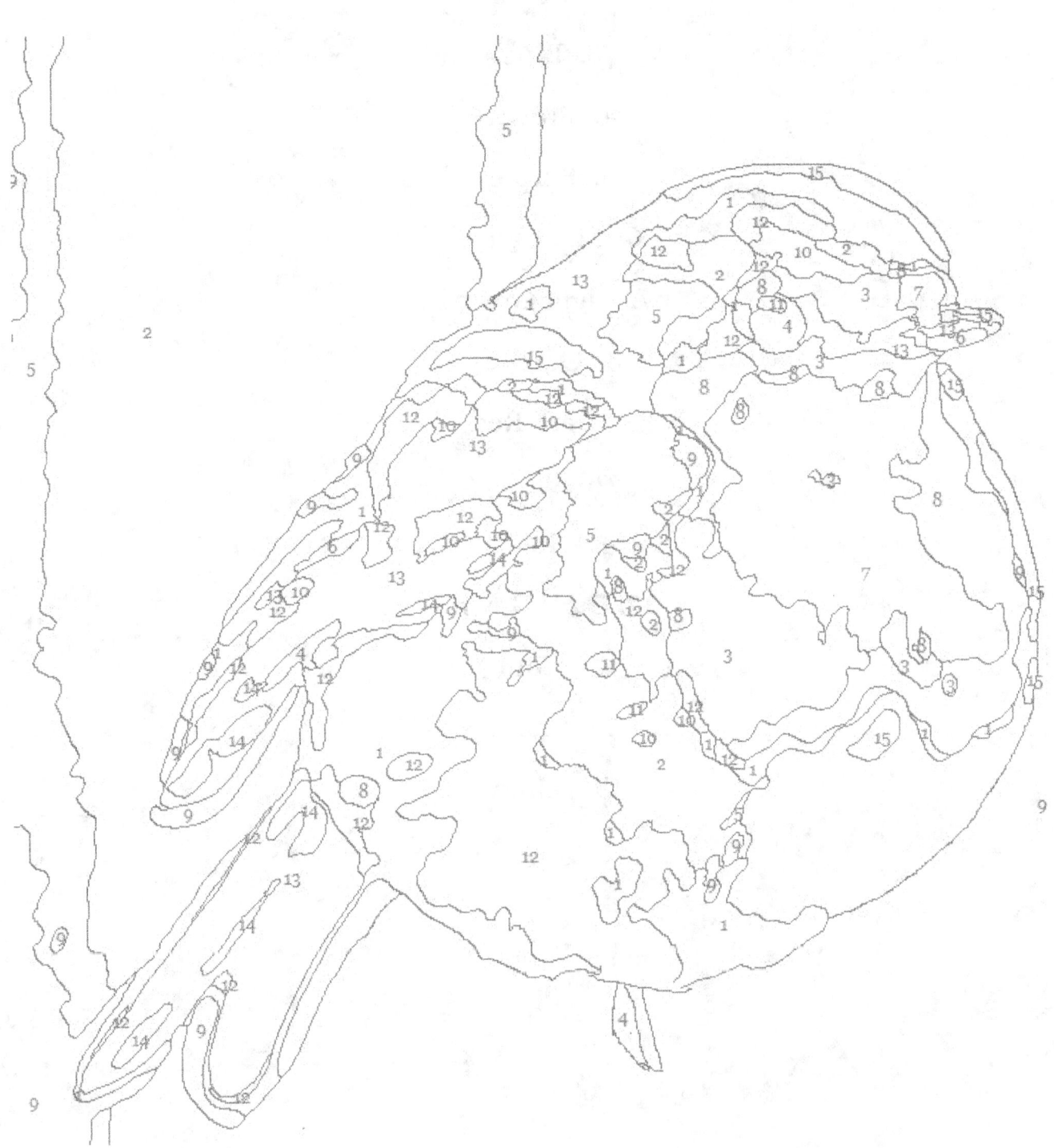

1. Black
2. Green
3. Blue
4. Brown
5. Purple
6. Light Blue
7. Light Green
8. Orange
9. Dark Red
10. Pink
11. Red
12. Dark Green
13. Gold
14. Violet
15. Yellow

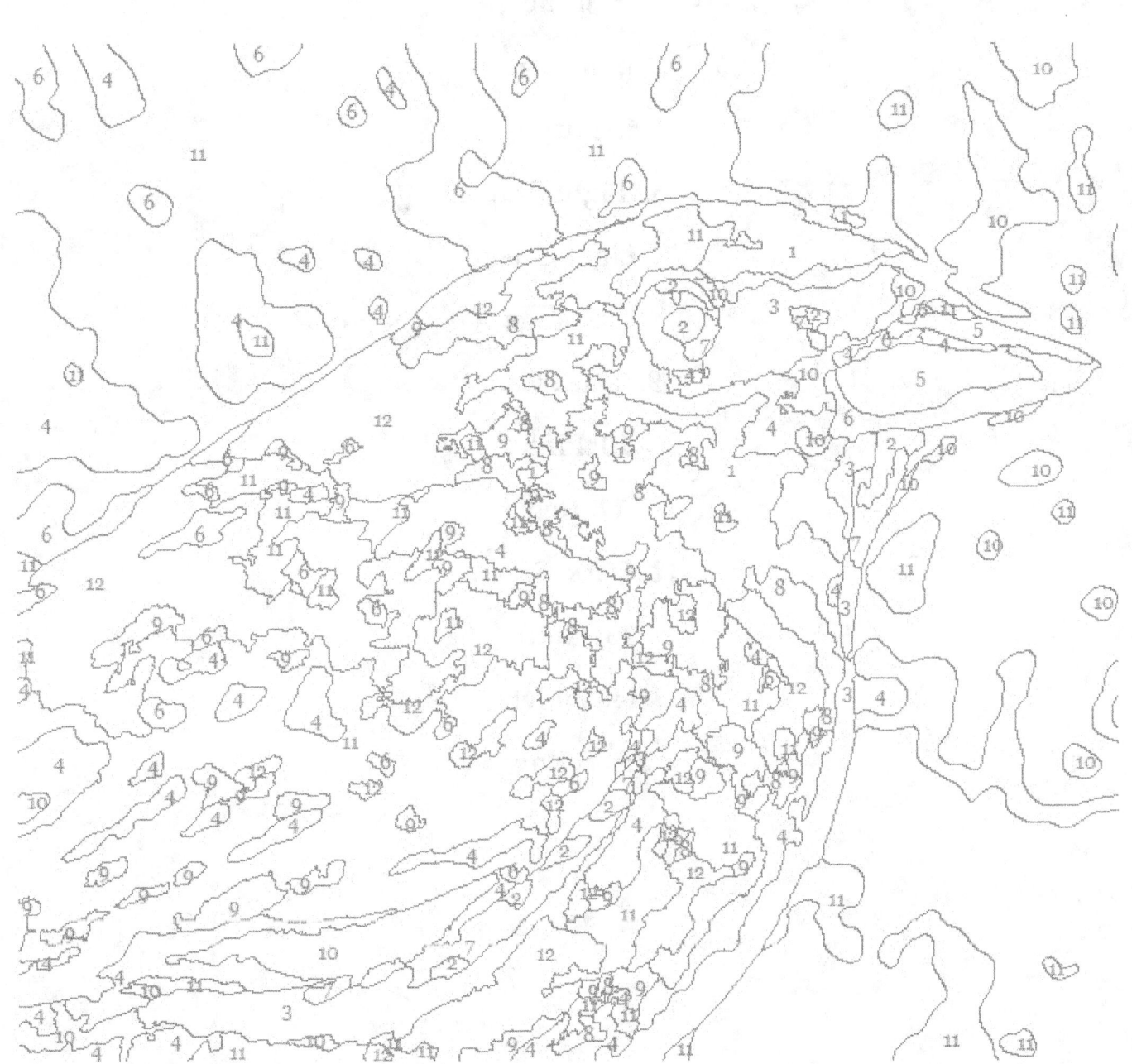

1. Black
2. Green
3. Blue
4. Brown
5. Purple
6. Light Blue
7. Light Green
8. Orange
9. Dark Red
10. Pink
11. Red
12. Dark Green
13. Gold
14. Violet
15. Yellow

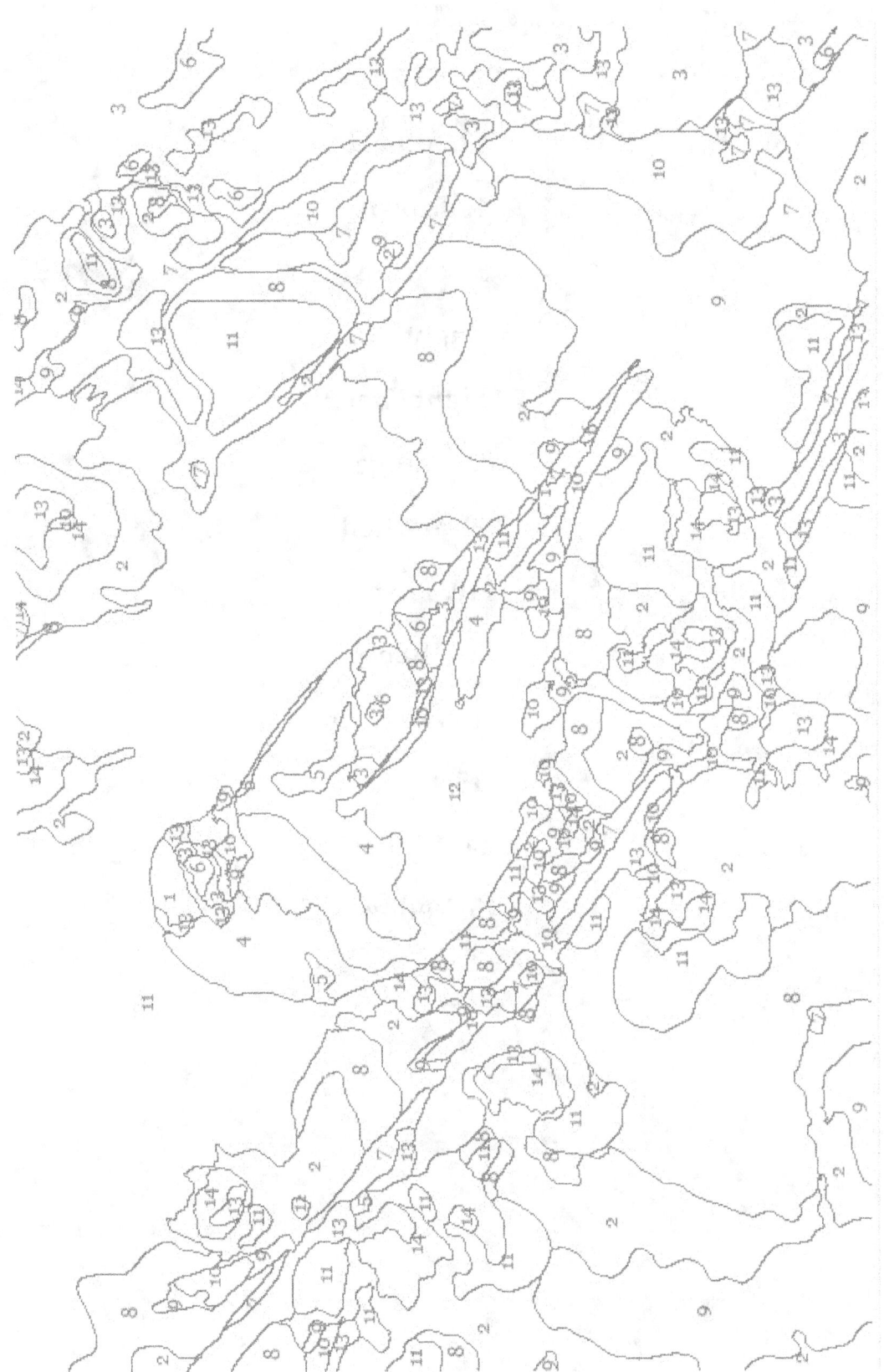

1. Black
2. Green
3. Blue
4. Brown
5. Purple
6. Light Blue
7. Light Green
8. Orange
9. Dark Red
10. Pink
11. Red
12. Dark Green
13. Gold
14. Violet
15. Yellow

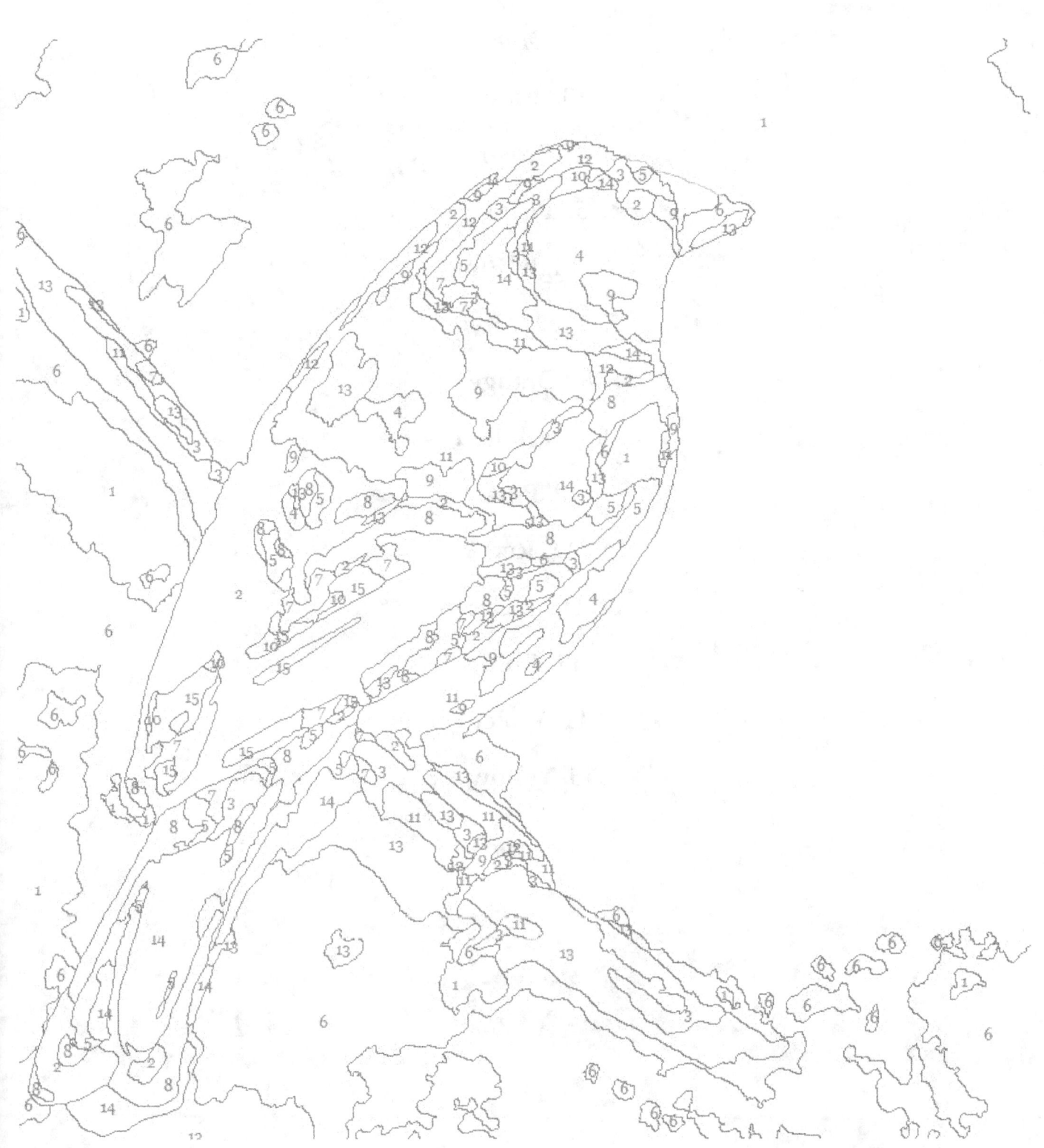

1. Black
2. Green
3. Blue
4. Brown
5. Purple
6. Light Blue
7. Light Green
8. Orange
9. Dark Red
10. Pink
11. Red
12. Dark Green
13. Gold
14. Violet
15. Yellow

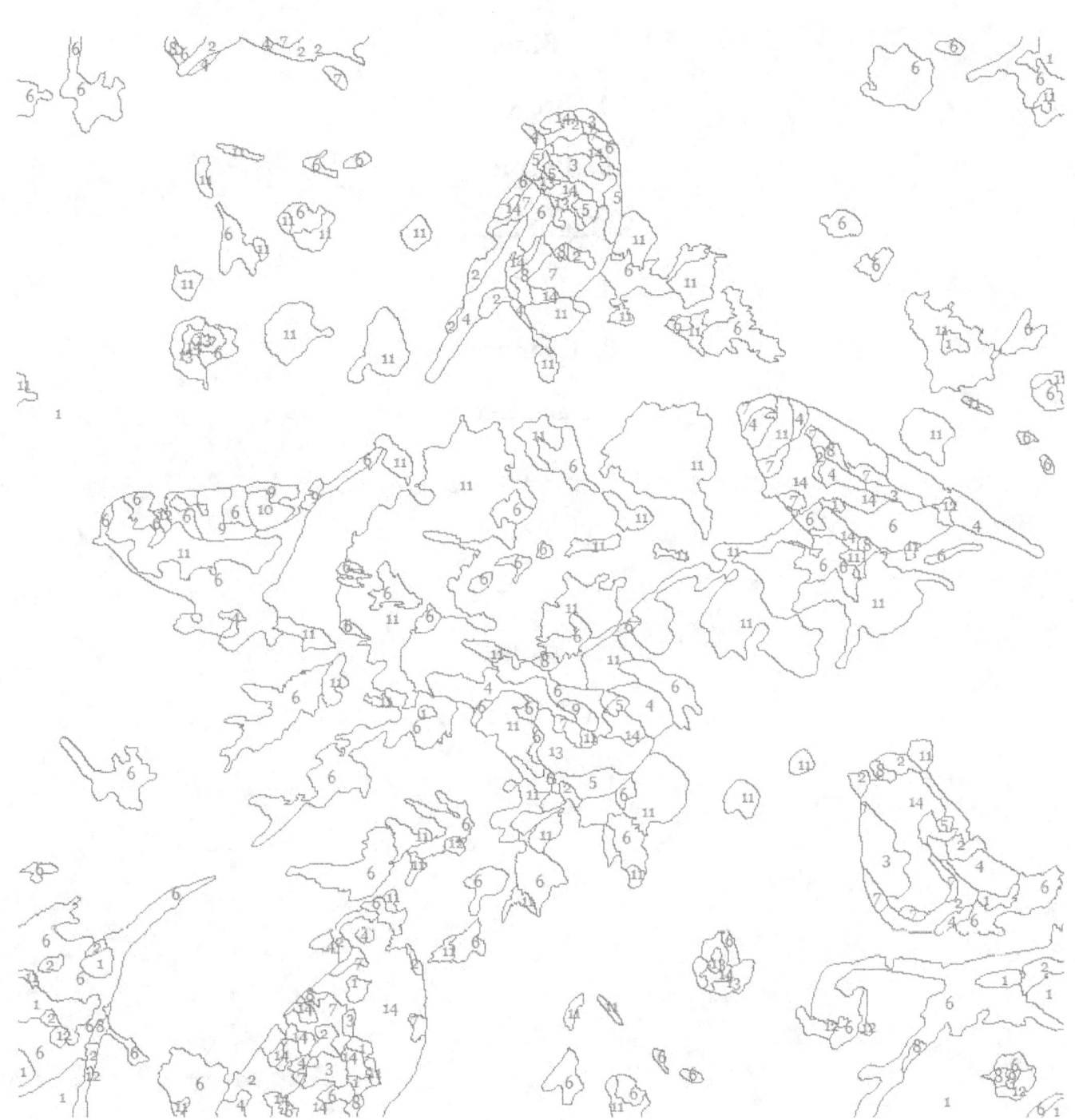

1. Black
2. Green
3. Blue
4. Brown
5. Purple
6. Light Blue
7. Light Green
8. Orange
9. Dark Red
10. Pink
11. Red
12. Dark Green
13. Gold
14. Violet
15. Yellow

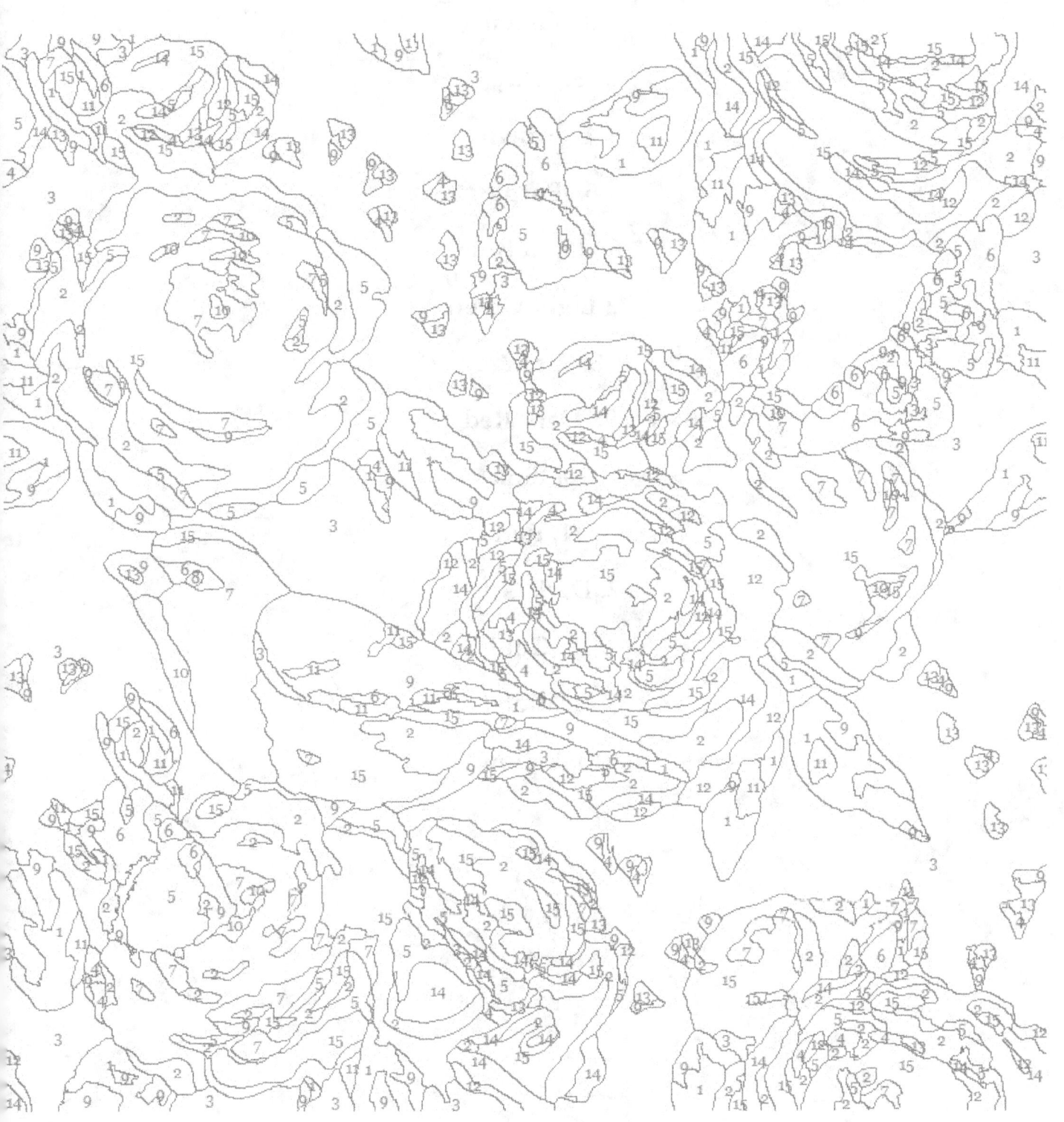

1. Black
2. Green
3. Blue
4. Brown
5. Purple
6. Light Blue
7. Light Green
8. Orange
9. Dark Red
10. Pink
11. Red
12. Dark Green
13. Gold
14. Violet
15. Yellow

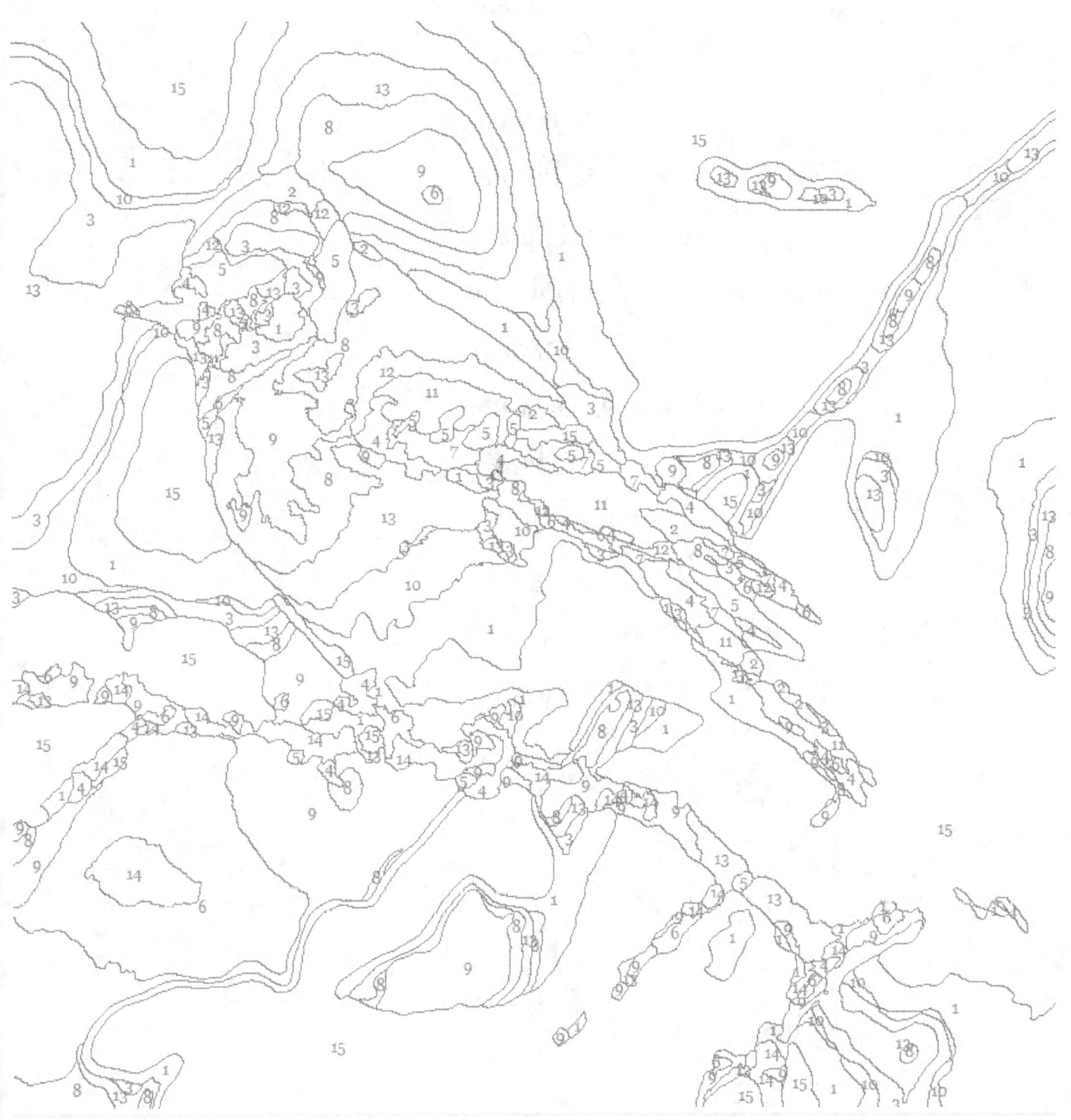

1. Black
2. Green
3. Blue
4. Brown
5. Purple
6. Light Blue
7. Light Green
8. Orange
9. Dark Red
10. Pink
11. Red
12. Dark Green
13. Gold
14. Violet
15. Yellow

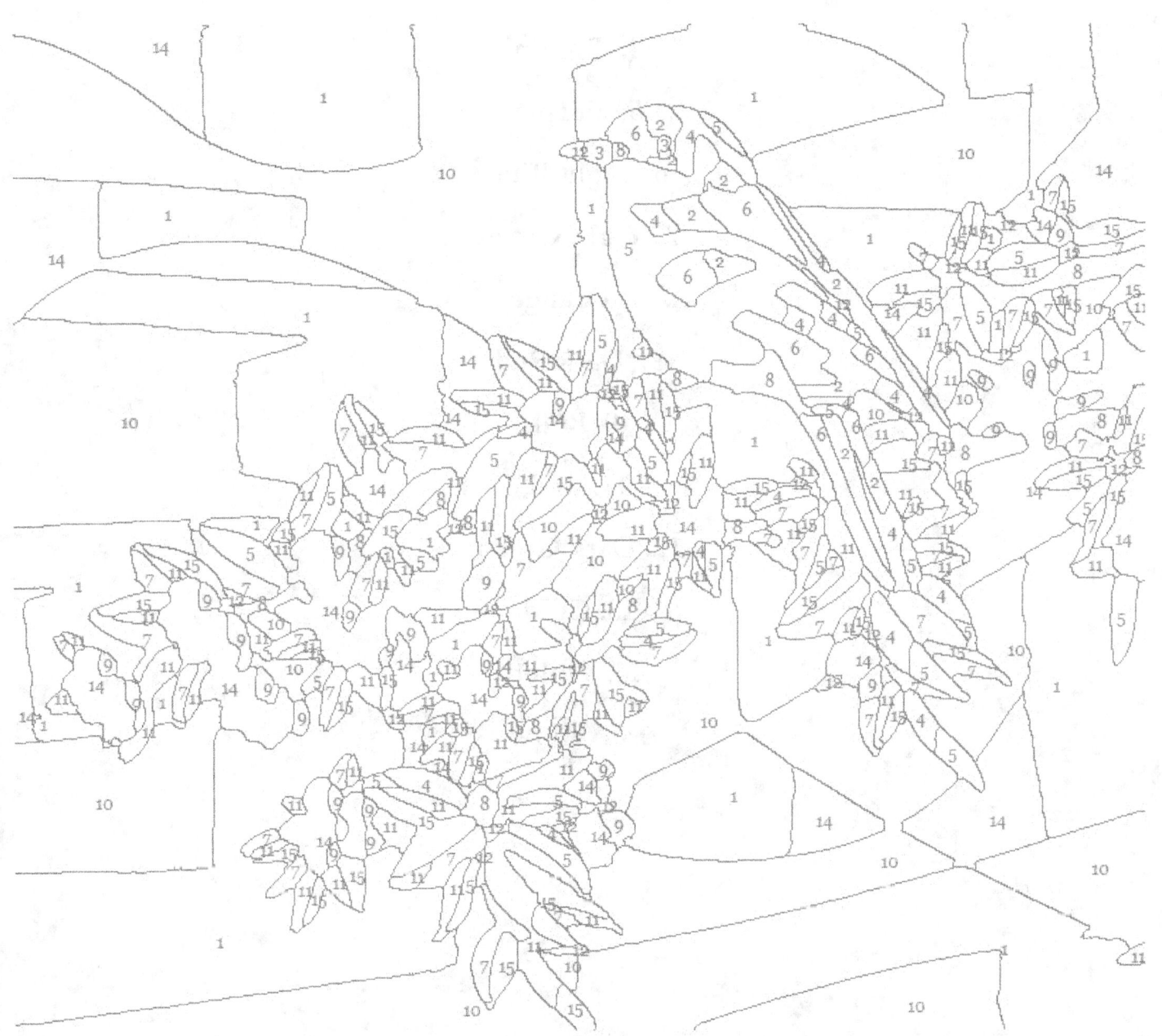

1. Black
2. Green
3. Blue
4. Brown
5. Purple
6. Light Blue
7. Light Green
8. Orange
9. Dark Red
10. Pink
11. Red
12. Dark Green
13. Gold
14. Violet
15. Yellow

1. Black
2. Green
3. Blue
4. Brown
5. Purple
6. Light Blue
7. Light Green
8. Orange
9. Dark Red
10. Pink
11. Red
12. Dark Green
13. Gold
14. Violet
15. Yellow

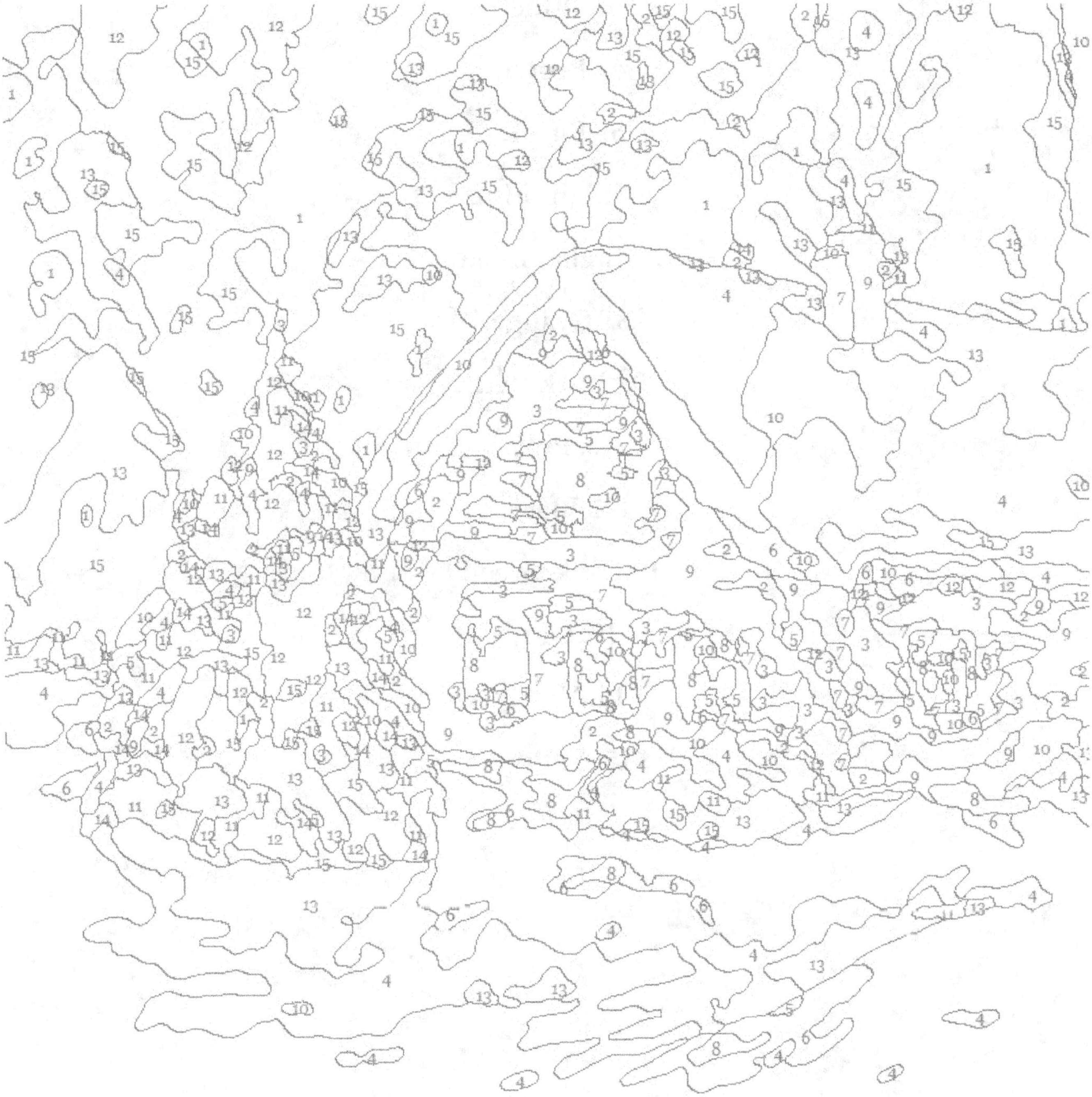

1. Red
2. Green
3. Blue
4. Brown
5. Purple
6. Light Blue
7. Light Green
8. Orange
9. Dark Red
10. Pink
11. Black
12. Dark Green
13. Gold
14. Violet
15. Yellow

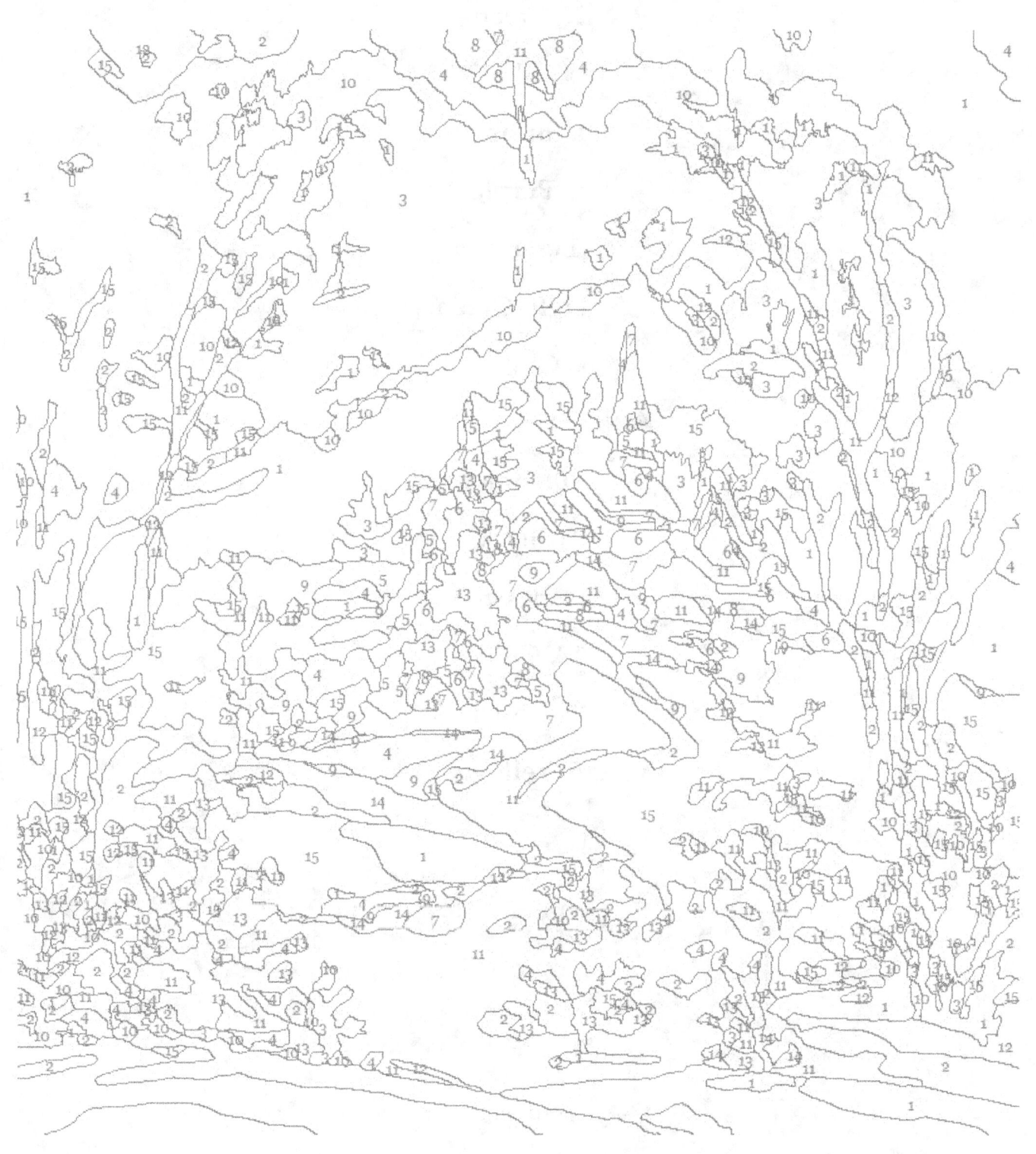

1. Red
2. Green
3. Blue
4. Brown
5. Purple
6. Light Blue
7. Light Green
8. Orange
9. Dark Red
10. Pink
11. Black
12. Dark Green
13. Gold
14. Violet
15. Yellow

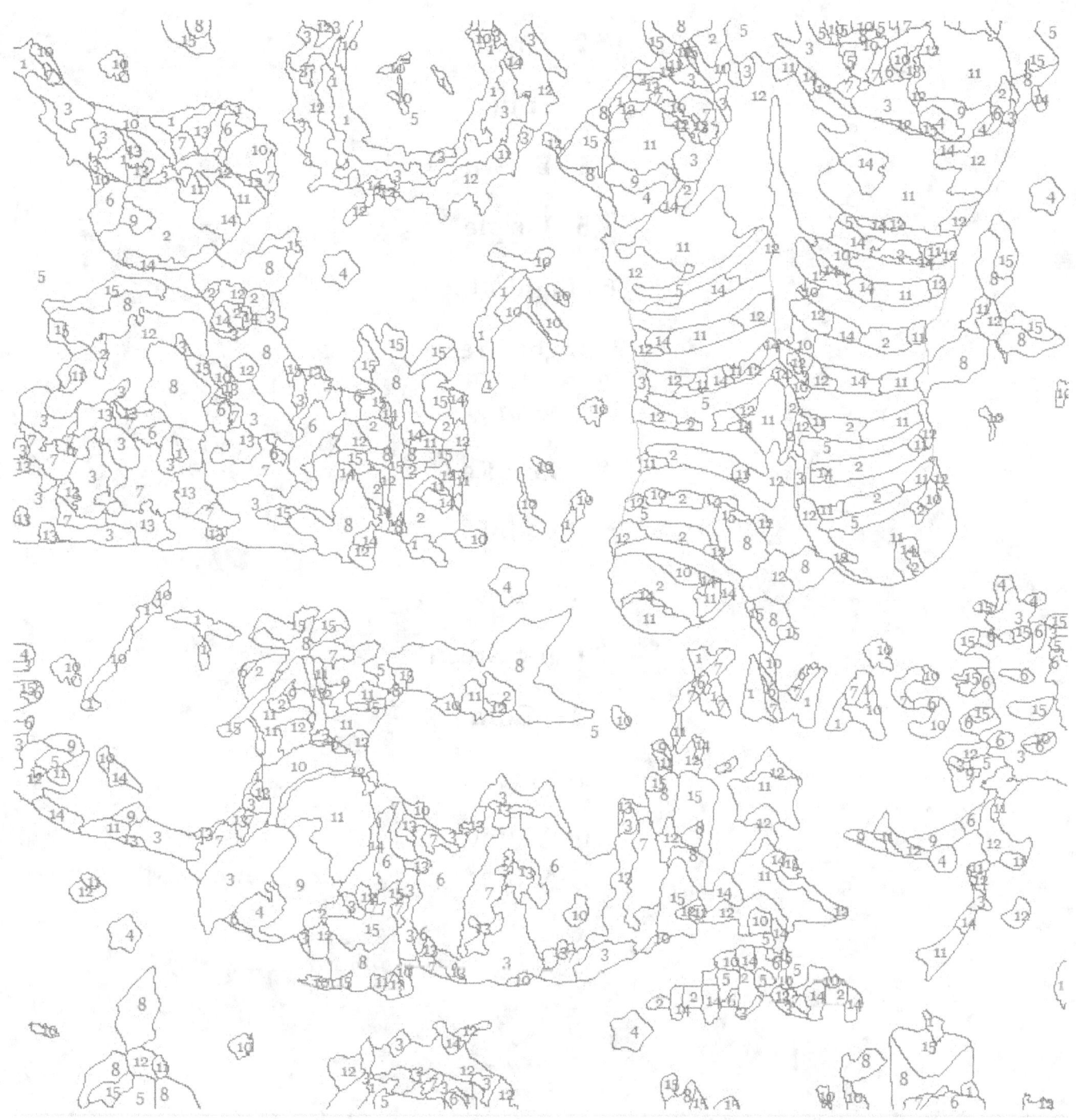

1. Red
2. Green
3. Blue
4. Brown
5. Purple
6. Light Blue
7. Light Green
8. Orange
9. Dark Red
10. Pink
11. Black
12. Dark Green
13. Gold
14. Violet
15. Yellow

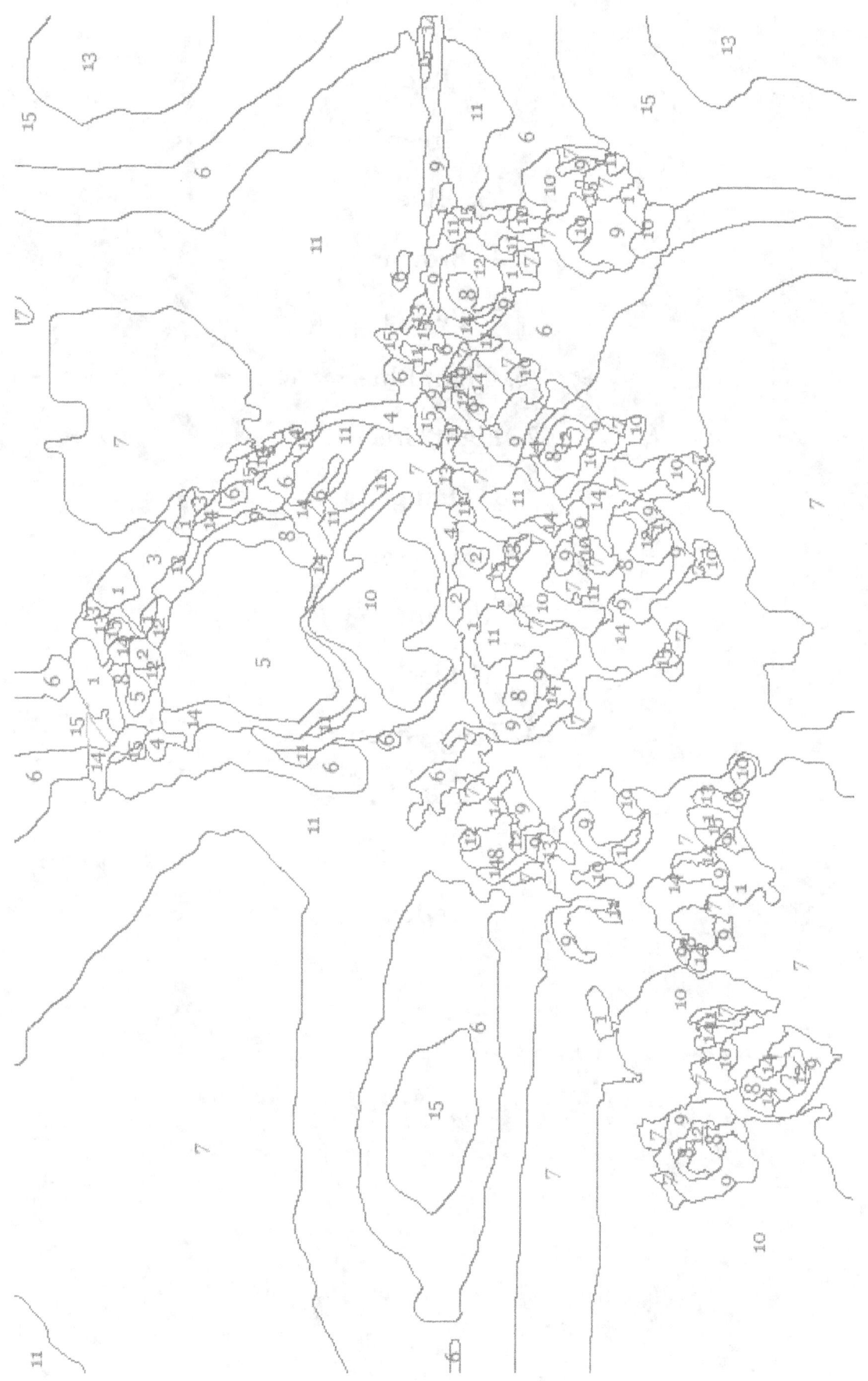

1. Red
2. Green
3. Blue
4. Brown
5. Purple
6. Light Blue
7. Light Green
8. Orange
9. Dark Red
10. Pink
11. Black
12. Dark Green
13. Gold
14. Violet
15. Yellow

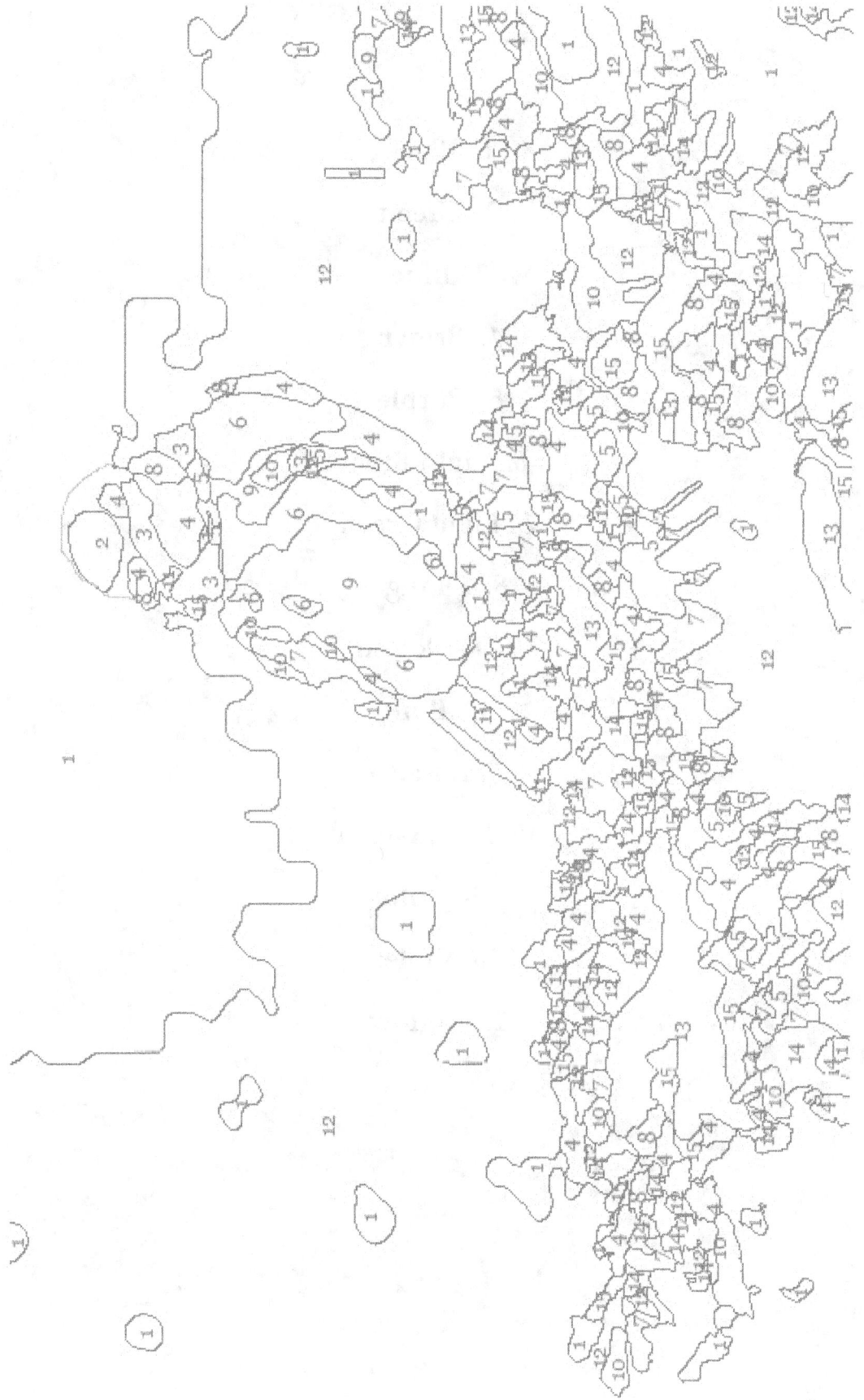

1. Black
2. Green
3. Blue
4. Brown
5. Purple
6. Light Blue
7. Light Green
8. Orange
9. Dark Red
10. Pink
11. Red
12. Dark Green
13. Gold
14. Violet
15. Yellow

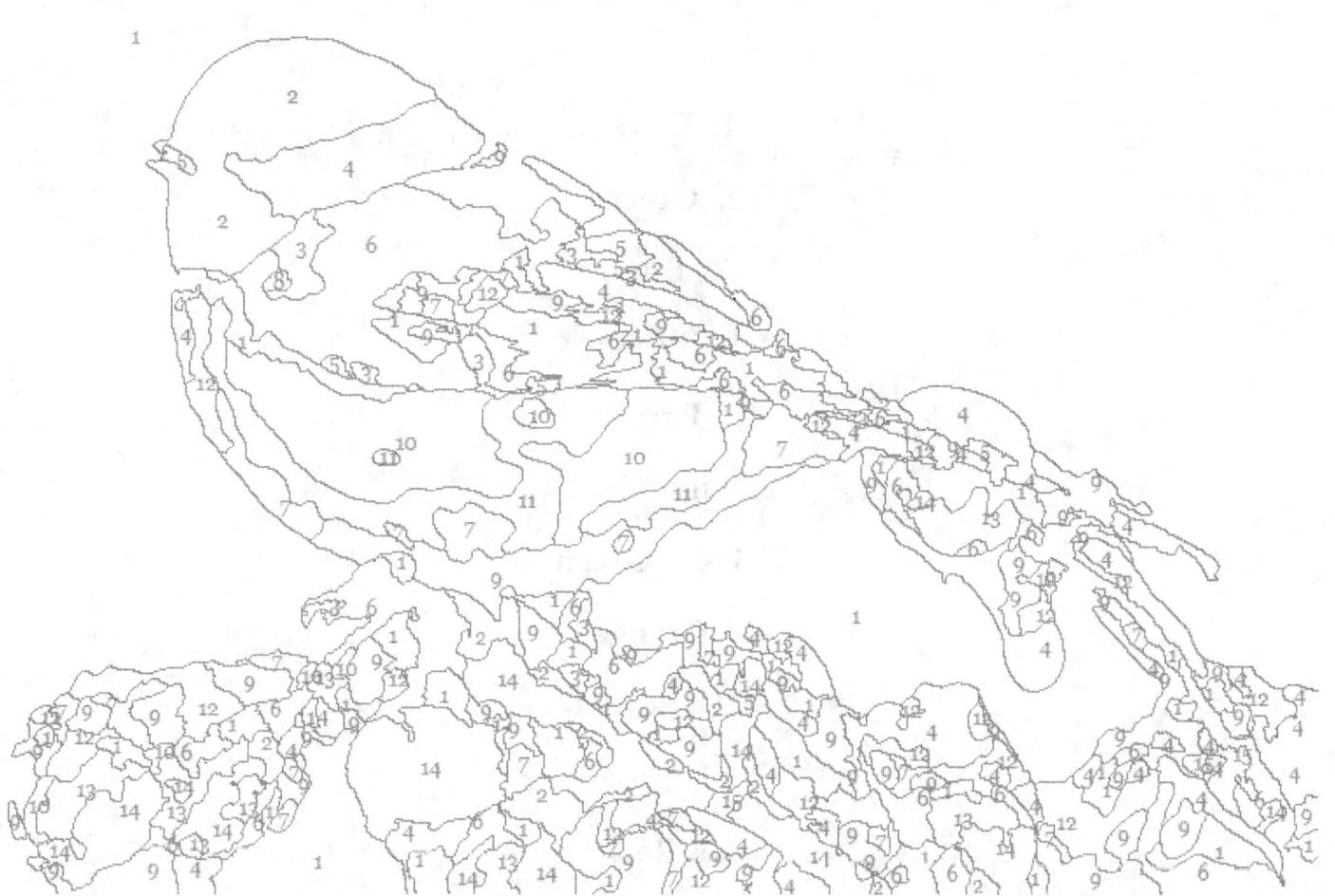

1. Black
2. Green
3. Blue
4. Brown
5. Purple
6. Light Blue
7. Light Green
8. Orange
9. Dark Red
10. Pink
11. Red
12. Dark Green
13. Gold
14. Violet
15. Yellow

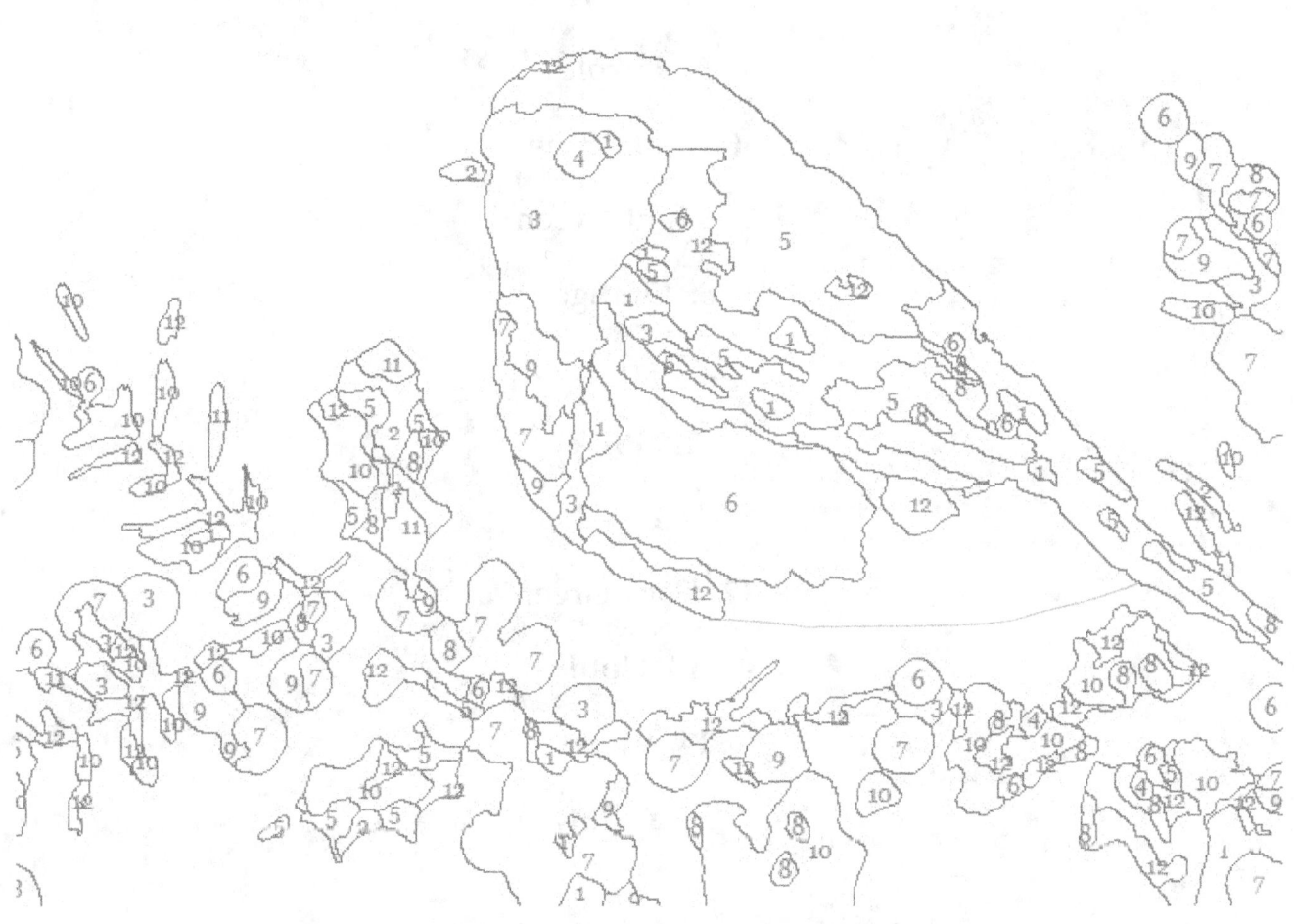

1. Black
2. Green
3. Blue
4. Brown
5. Purple
6. Light Blue
7. Light Green
8. Orange
9. Dark Red
10. Pink
11. Red
12. Dark Green
13. Gold
14. Violet
15. Yellow

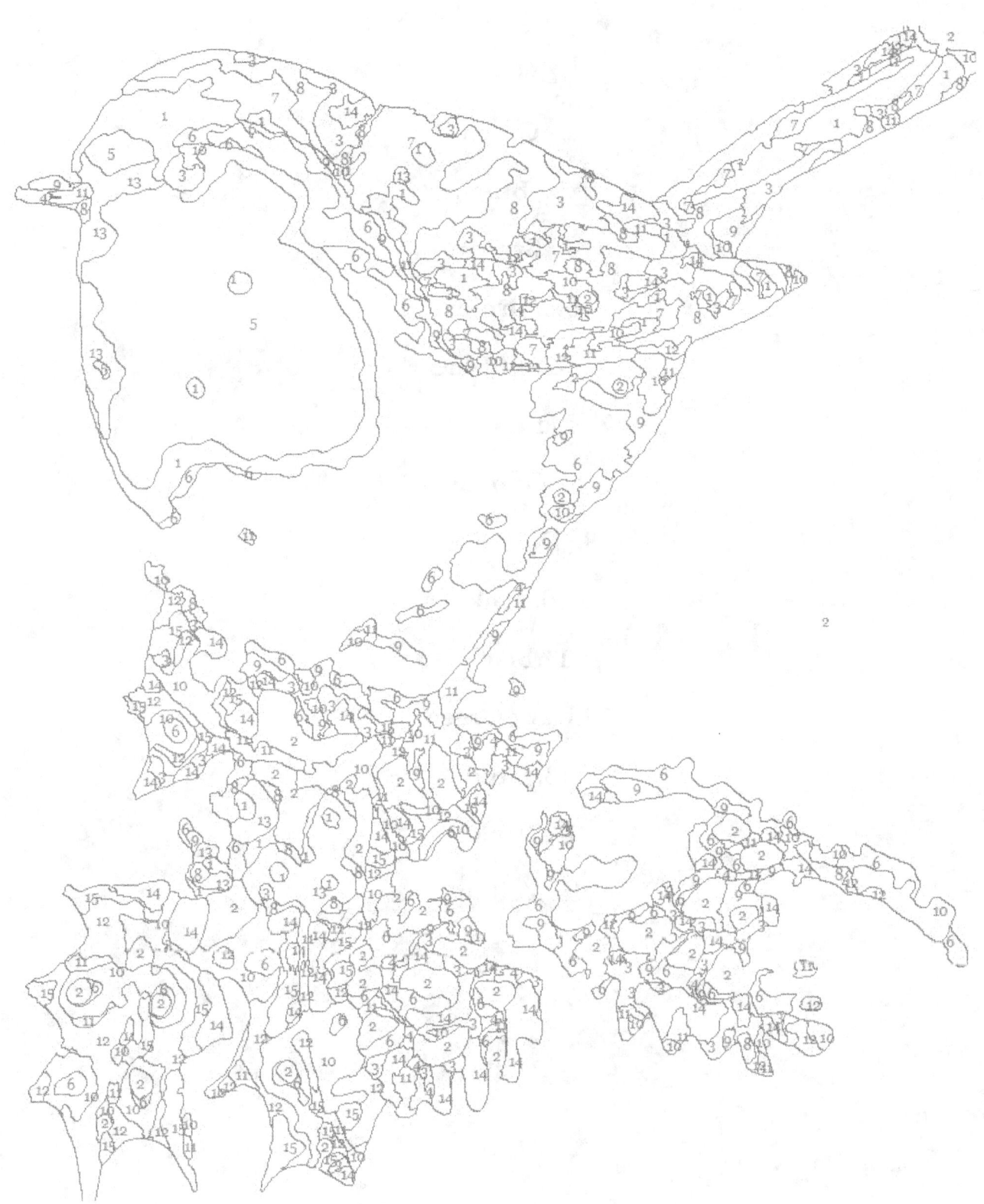

1. Red
2. Green
3. Blue
4. Brown
5. Purple
6. Light Blue
7. Light Green
8. Orange
9. Dark Red
10. Pink
11. Black
12. Dark Green
13. Gold
14. Violet
15. Yellow

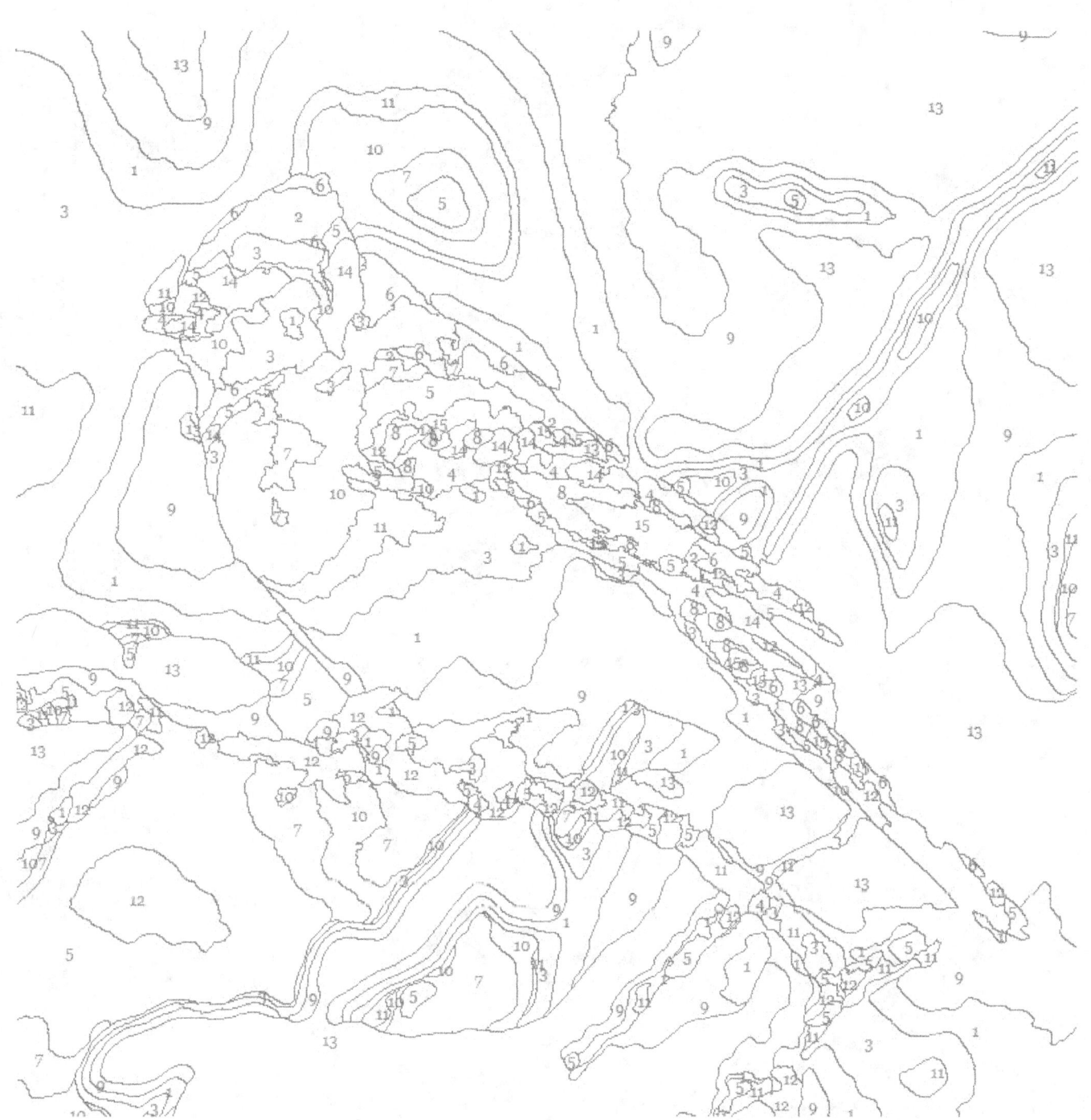

Bonus Dot to Dot Bird Puzzles

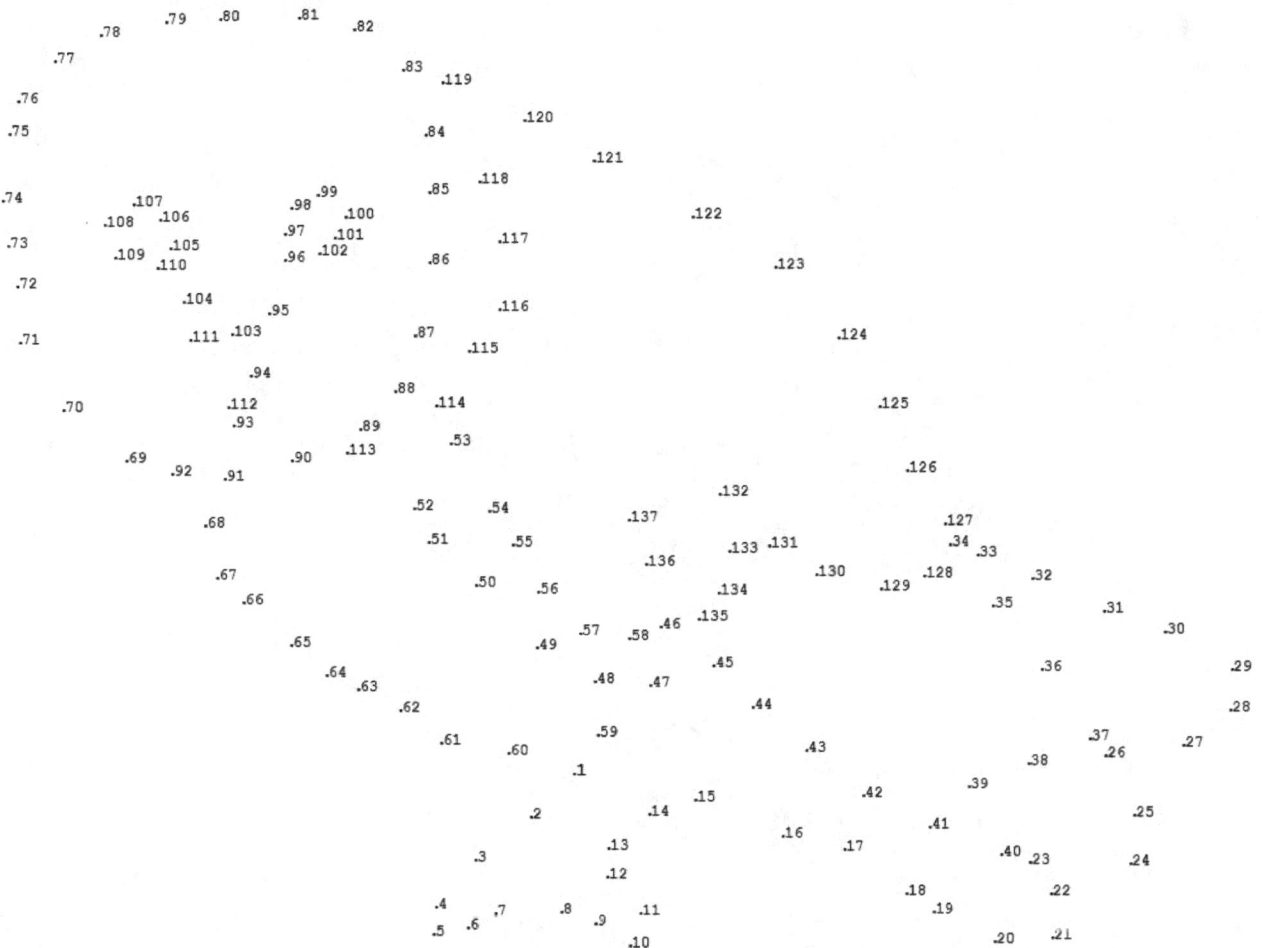

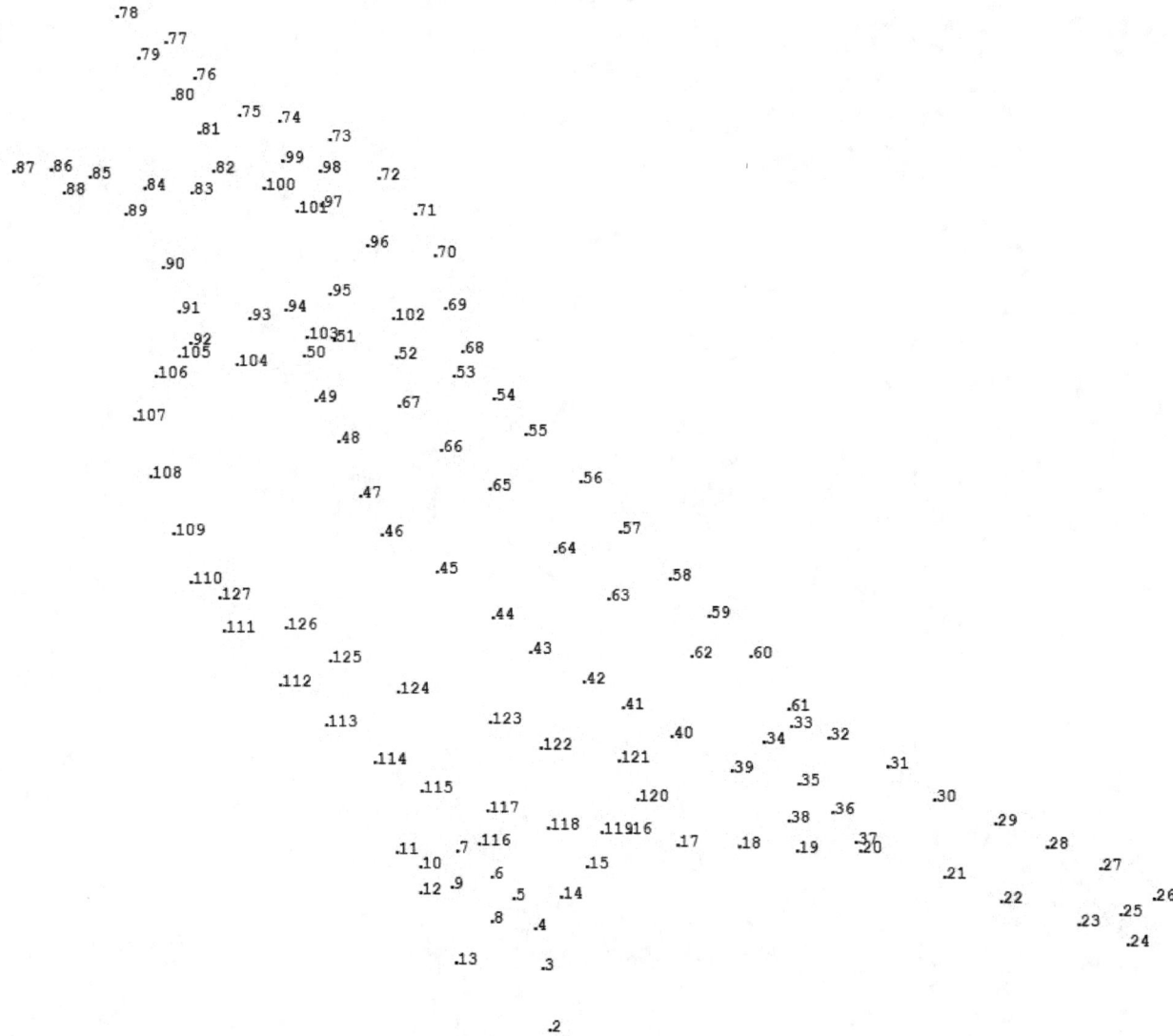

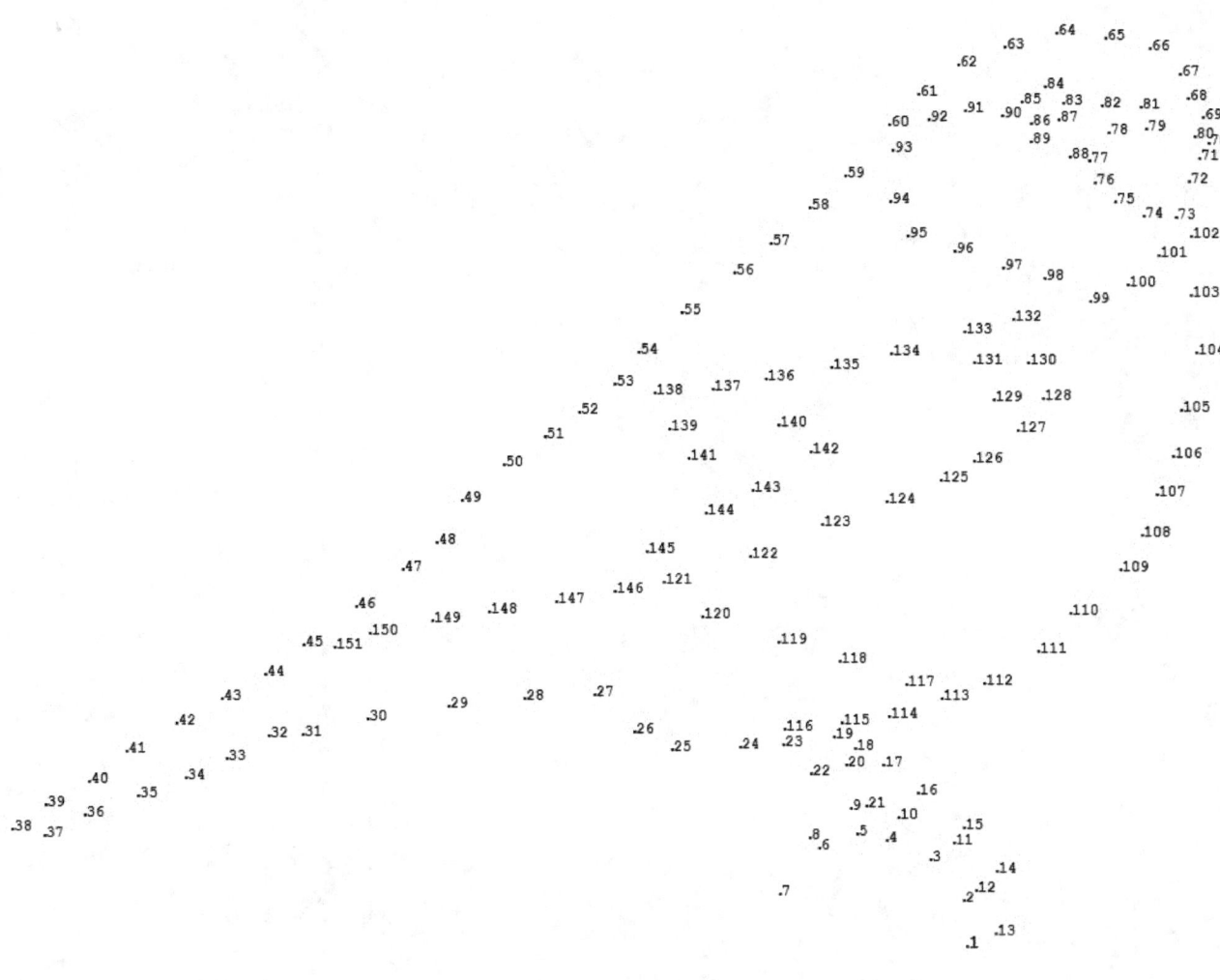

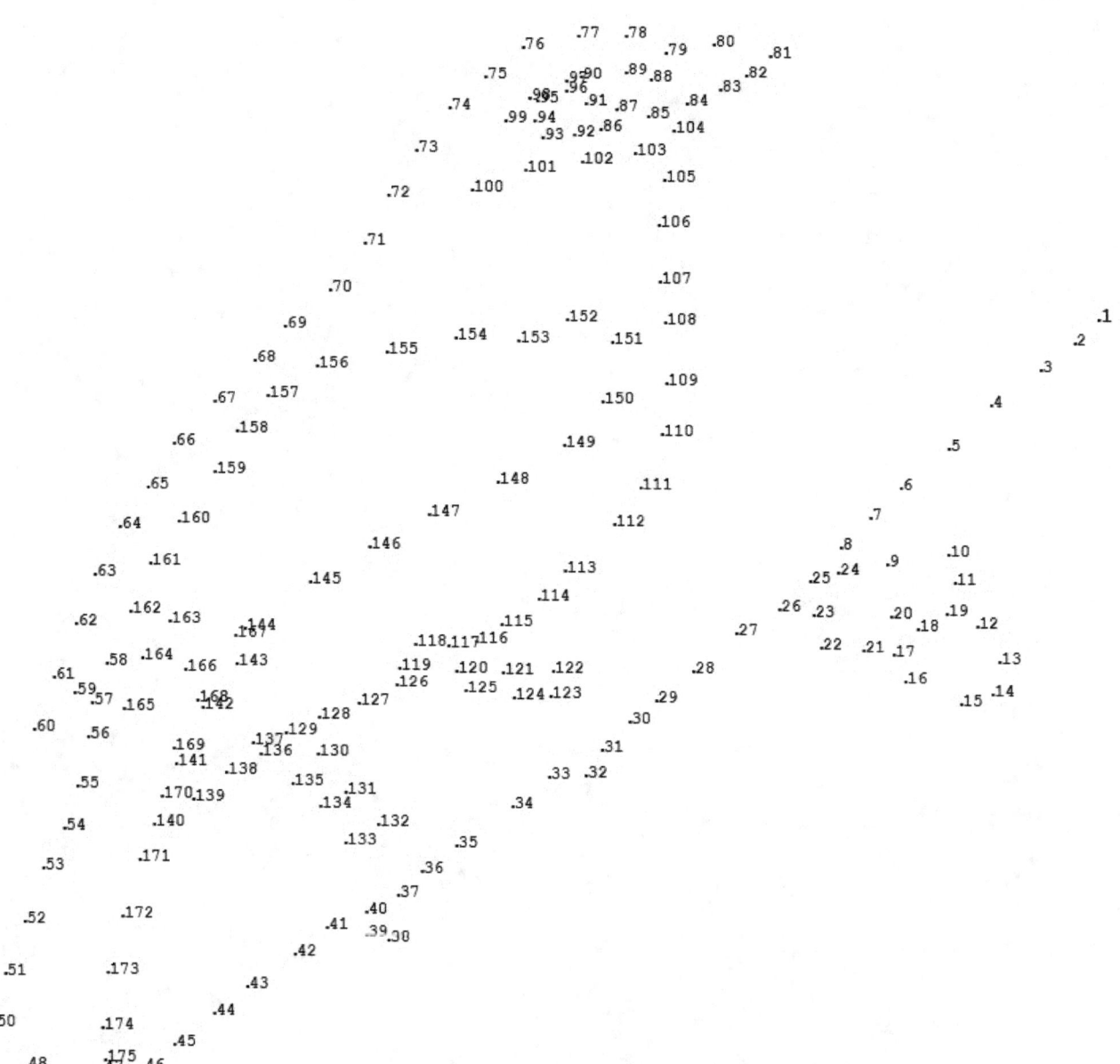

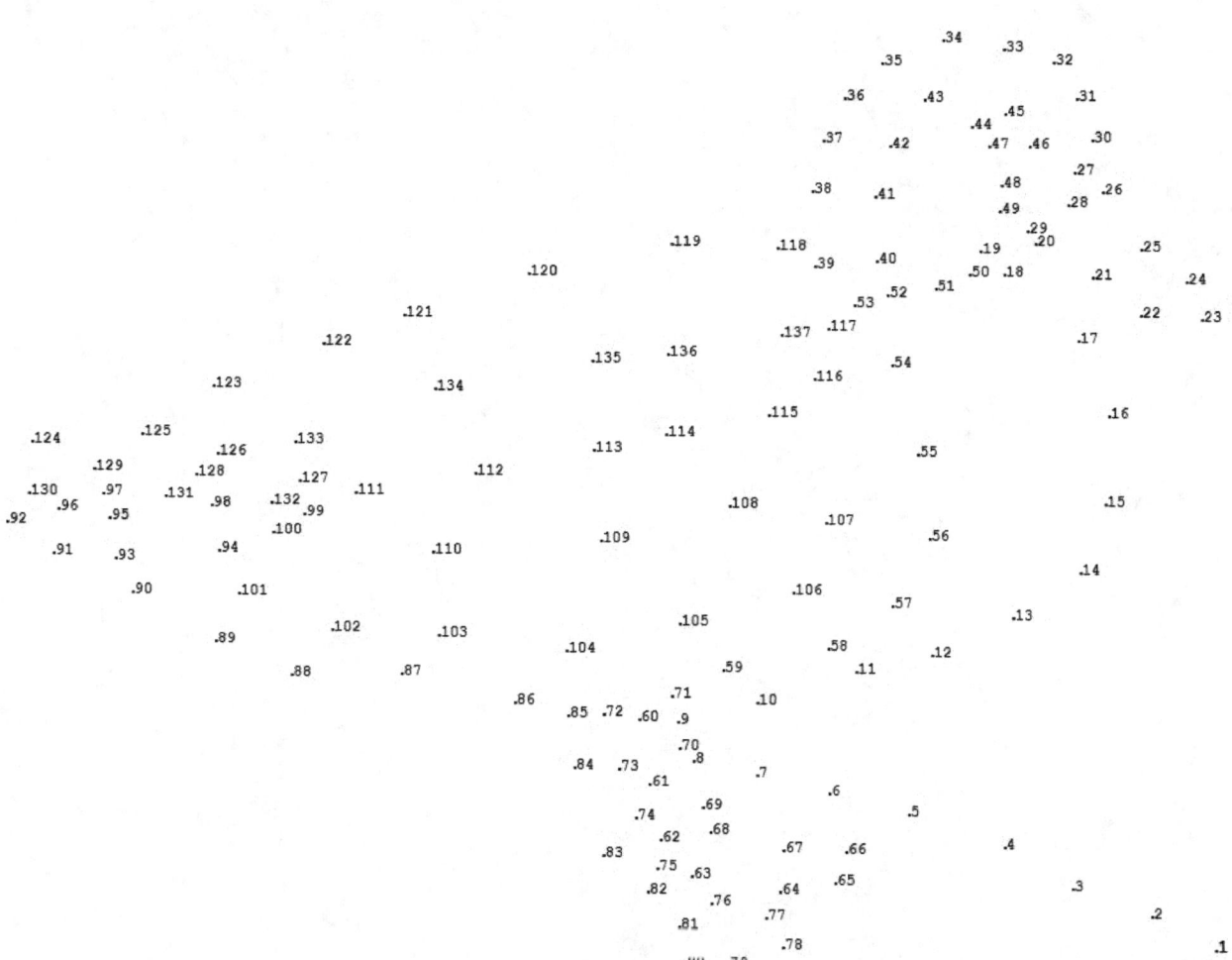

www.ingramcontent.com/pod-product-compliance
Lightning Source LLC
Chambersburg PA
CBHW081621220526
45468CB00010B/2976